GW01607788

TORTOISE TALES

Tortoise Tales

Sheila Groves

VICTORY PRESS

EASTBOURNE

ISBN 0 85476 246 9

Text and cover illustrations
by Diane Matthes

Printed in Great Britain for
VICTORY PRESS (Evangelical Publishers Ltd)
Lottbridge Drove, Eastbourne, E. Sussex BN23 6NT
by Fletcher & Son Ltd. Norwich

CONTENTS

Tortoise Tales

1

The Greatest of all the Birds

Take-Your-Time was a very new little tortoise. He hadn't been in the world very long, and he was curious about everything. One day he poked his head out of his shell and said

"Mummy, who is the cleverest person in all the world?"

"Why, your great-grandpapa, More-Haste-Less-Speed," she replied, scrubbing some grass

stains off his shell. "And how often have I told you not to play in the wet grass?"

The next day – although the grass was still wet – Take-Your-Time set out to look for his great-grandpapa, More - Haste - Less - Speed. After a long time he found him sitting under a sycamore tree, having his after dinner snooze.

Take-Your-Time stared.

His great-grandpapa was very old, and gnarled like the tree, and had a funny bumpy shell. And in the bumpiest bit of his shell was what looked like a keyhole.

"Don't stare, it's very rude," said a gruff sleepy voice.

Take-Your-Time jumped.

"I'm sorry, great-grandpapa. I thought you were asleep. Great-grandpapa, what do you keep in your shell?"

More-Haste-Less-Speed sighed, and said goodbye to his after dinner snooze. "Fetch me my keys," he said.

Take-Your-Time unhooked the big bunch of keys hanging on the sycamore tree, and unlocked the little door in his great-grandpapa's shell. Then, very carefully, he pulled out a big bundle of leaves.

"What are they?" he asked, putting the bundle down gently.

"Stories," said More-Haste-Less-Speed indignantly. "Can't you read?"

Take-Your-Time shook his head sadly. "Will you read me one, great-grandpapa?"

More-Haste-Less-Speed looked

pleased. He shuffled around a bit, pulled out his spectacles from another bump, put them on and glared at his great-grandson over the top of them. Then he pulled out a leaf and began:

This one is about Cock. Perhaps you won't have met him - but you'll have heard him, every morning, cock-a-doodling; just because he gets up early, he thinks everyone else ought to as well. He lives in a little house in the corner of the farmyard. Just behind his house, down in the hedge, lives a sparrow. Not much to look at - not like the cock with his flashy red crest - but a nice quiet little chap.

Well, one day the cock woke up very early. He stretched, flew up onto the roof of his house and strutted up and down.

"Doodle-doo!" he crowed. "I sing so beautifully that the sun comes out and everyone gets up to listen to me! If it wasn't for me, people would stay in bed all day, and no one would do any work.

Ca-aaw! I'm the greatest of all the birds!"

And he puffed out his chest and sang and sang and sang, till the whole village put its hands over its ears and buried its head in the bedclothes to try to get to sleep again.

But when the sparrow woke up he was very sad.

"Oh dear," he said. "There are so many other sparrows just like me; I'm a very common sort of bird. I'm not beautiful and I'm no good to anyone. I can't wake people up, like the cock, or make them laugh like the cuckoo. I can't sing to them like the nightingale or have my picture on their Christmas cards like the robin. I'm the poorest of all the birds!"

That afternoon a little girl walked through the farmyard. She was feeling very lonely. "I wish there was someone to talk to me," she thought.

But all the animals were asleep in the hot sun. Only the cock and the sparrow were awake.

The cock saw the little girl as she sat down sadly on a stone, and he thought "I could have shown her what a beautiful voice I've got; but I sang so loudly this morning that I've lost my song and my throat is sore. In fact, it hurts so much, I think I'll go back to bed."

And off he flew.

Then the sparrow heard the little girl crying. "Poor thing," he thought. "What can have happened to make her cry like that?"

And he flew onto the stone beside her and chirped softly.

The little girl heard him and turned round. Then she dried her tears. "You came to talk to me," she said, smiling. "Thank you. I like you much better than everyone else!"

The sparrow blinked. Had she said that to him? To him, the poorest of all the birds? Suddenly it didn't matter any more that he couldn't wake people up, or that he'd never had his picture on a Christmas card.

"So you see," More-Haste-Less-Speed removed his glasses and put the story away carefully, "it doesn't matter who you are or how much noise you make -"

"Or even if you can't read," interrupted Take-Your-Time hopefully.

". . . how much noise you make, as I was saying," his great-grand-papa continued severely. "It's where your heart is, that's what matters in the Long Run."

"The Long Run?" enquired Take-Your-Time anxiously.

But his great-grandpapa's head had disappeared once more into his shell, and Take-Your-Time took the hint.

Did you know that Jesus told a story like this one?

It was about a man who went to church all the time and told everybody how good he was: and about another man, who knew he'd done lots of things that were wrong. Jesus said that God was pleased with the second man, because he knew he had to ask God to forgive him for the wrong things; but the first man thought he was good enough already.

Who do you like better in the story, the cock or the sparrow?

If we do things to help other people - help them when they're busy, cheer them up if they're by themselves or ill - then we will make Jesus pleased.

Do you think Jesus was pleased with the cock?

2

Nuts for Tomorrow

"This," said More-Haste-Less-Speed, reluctantly taking the bunch of sycamore keys, "is becoming a habit."

"I didn't come for a story." Take-Your-Time was waving his head backwards and forwards in agitation.

"Oh." More-Haste-Less-Speed was about to withdraw in a huff, but Take-Your-Time said hastily "Don't go, great-grandpapa. I had nightmares all last night.

"Dear me, what about?" said the elderly tortoise more kindly.

"The Long Run," Take-Your-Time licked his lips. "Great-grandpapa, what *is* it? And will all the tortoises end up *very* far behind?"

A curious trembling took hold of More-Haste-Less-Speed, slight at first, but growing stronger and stronger, until a large bunch of stories were shaken out and Take-Your-Time had to amble hurriedly after them.

"Ho, ho, he hee, ha, ha!" Tears were running down his great-grandpapa's cheeks when Take-Your-Time returned with the stories. "Bless my soul! Haven't laughed so much for a long time. Bless the lad!"

Take-Your-Time pointed out - respectfully but with a good deal of heat - that his nightmare had not been At All Funny.

"Of course not," More-Haste-Less-Speed pulled himself together and summoned a passing tortoiseshell butterfly to wipe away his tears with her wing. "The Long Run. Yes. Well, what you do today and tomorrow - breakfast, playing in the wet grass, a stroll and maybe a story, a little polishing of the shell once or twice a week - all that's what you might call the Short Run. Hmm. Would you mind scratching my head for me - no, a little to the right?"

Take-Your-Time obliged.

"And the Long Run?" he reminded his great-grandpapa half an hour later.

"I was coming to that," said More-Haste-Less-Speed severely. "Don't *rush* me." After several moments, he continued. "The

Long Run isn't what happens today or tomorrow or even next week; it's what happens months and years away. *And,*" his voice dropped to a whisper and Take-Your-Time had to come very close, "*and* when one day we'll lose these clumsy old shells and have new golden ones with twice as much room for stories!"

Take-Your-Time opened his eyes very wide.

"But how -"

His great-grandpapa held up a foot for silence.

"That's enough thinking for one day. Pass me a story and sit quiet and listen, there's a good lad."

His great-grandson picked out a pretty golden-brown story and settled into a patch of clover.

"Ah yes," More-Haste-Less-

Speed peered through his spectacles: About Knut. Now, you know what squirrels are like, and Knut was no exception. All day, every day, hazelnuts, beechnuts, peanuts that People had dropped; and what does he do with them? Eat them? Oh no. Hoards them.

One day his second cousin Cyril scampered around.

"I say, old man, got a few beechnuts to spare? It's the wife - very poorly, you know, and I haven't had a moment to go out collecting."

"Sorry," Knut hardly paused on his way down the tree. "My Beech Grove Storehouse has just been filled and sealed up. I'll let you have some when it's opened next month. Can't stop now - only

another five fistfuls and Hazel Corner Hoards will be full too!"

Three days later, Cyril was back. "Don't bother," he said. "Scilla's dead."

"Oh!" Knut was shocked - and a little ashamed. "But if I'd known she would die - why didn't you tell me?"

But Cyril had gone.

Knut soon recovered, and went on collecting. Peanut Pantry was nearly full now, and he'd started an overflow hoard in his own tree. Life was busy, oh so busy, and Knut chattered happily to himself as he worked.

Then one day Cyril came back and stood under his tree.

"Why are you doing all that?" he asked.

Knut stopped in surprise. "But my dear fellow, everyone does. I

Jesus told a story about a man who was like Knut; he collected lots and lots of things so that one day he wouldn't have to work: he could just enjoy all the things he had. But that very night, the man died, so he couldn't enjoy any of them.

Jesus said that we should be kind and generous with the things we have.

What do you think Cyril meant when he said "What about the

hungry squirrels?"

More-Haste-Less-Speed was dreaming of the day when he would have a new golden shell. When we die, Jesus says that if we believe in him, we shall have new bodies and we will live with him in heaven for ever.

another story. "More to it than just reading," he remarked. "You just listen." He cleared his throat and began:

Moldwin was very learned, and he lived under a molehill - or rather, half a dozen molehills - in the shade of one of the biggest castles in Wales. Learned he was, and learned he looked, in his dusty smoking jacket and gold-rimmed spectacles.

He had the largest collection of stories - from The Books, you know - of anyone for miles around, and he read them every morning before breakfast and every evening before going to bed. He even took private pupils and taught them what was in the stories.

One day Moldwin heard foot-steps outside one of his front

doors. there was a light knock, and a little earth fell into the passage.

He had never seen his visitor before; he was a young mole - a student, Moldwin guessed, from his scruffy clothes and long fur - but he was very polite and spoke up nicely.

"I'm Werper," they shook hands. "They tell me you are very learned and know all the stories from The Books."

Moldwin invited him in ("Seems a sensible lad," he muttered) and showed him into the library. Werper looked round carefully, then nodded in approval.

"I see you have the complete collection of Cock stories," he said, "including the one about the porcupine - that's very rare."

think you were just a scruffy student -"

Moldwin blushed; how did he know? - "But which is more important?"

Moldwin looked lovingly round at all his piles of stories, and for a long time sat in his deep, moth-eaten chair, lost in thought. When

he finally looked up, Werper had gone.

For a moment, Moldwin was startled; he hadn't heard his visitor move. Then he shook his head, polished his spectacles, and set about re-arranging his gold and orange lion stories.

More-Haste-Less-Speed sat for a while without speaking. "So it's doing as well as reading, you see," he said at last. "A sad story," he added. "Moles are always so short-sighted."

"Do you mean they only see the Short Run?" asked Take-Your-Time.

"Yes, you could say that," said his great-grandpapa.

"But who was Werper?" insisted Take-Your-Time. "Was he - could he have been - did *he*- ?"

More-Haste-Less-Speed wagged

his head at his great-grandson and tucked his spectacles carefully into their bump. "There's some things in life." he said, "you have to make up your own mind about."

Take-Your-Time had to learn what was in The Books to find out how he should live; we must learn what is in the Bible.

Did you know that the Bible is really 66 books, written by about 40 different people? But although different people wrote it, it was God who told them all what to write and who made sure that none of it was lost.

Jesus told a story about a man who was beaten up and robbed; as he lay on the road, two religious men came by. They knew what was in the Bible; they knew it said that they should help the man. But they didn't. They passed by on the other side.

It's no good just *knowing* what the Bible says; we must *do* what it says. Jesus said that everyone who hears God's Word and obeys it will be happy.

Do you think Moldwin was happy?

4

Sherbert and Otter

"Really, we never see you nowadays," Take-Your-Time's mother didn't know whether to be pleased or sorry. "We'll have to invite your great-grandpapa to stay, you'll be wearing yourself out. Here, I'll write him a note."

She fetched a daisy leaf, wrote a few words and handed it to Take-Your-Time. "Don't forget to deliver it, now," she warned.

Take-Your-Time set off, and by tea time had found More-Haste-Less-Speed admiring himself in a

small pool of water near the sycamore tree.

"All these ripples," grumbled More-Haste-Less-Speed. "Makes me look like an old man!"

Take-Your-Time did not think it would be polite to point out that the surface of the pool was as smooth as a sheet of glass . . . Instead he said "Can I have another story, great-grandpapa? A really good one?"

"They're all good," said his great-grandpapa indignantly. "None of your cheap rubbish here - wouldn't give it houseroom. Now, let me see . . ."

It was a good hour later before they were ready to begin, as Take-Your-Time managed to drop the sycamore keys into the pool, so they had to wait for them to dry before they would work the lock.

But tortoises have all the time in the world, and a great deal of patience, so it didn't really matter.

"*Here* we are," More-Haste-Less-Speed carefully pulled out of the bump in his shell a large, golden leaf. It was evidently quite old and very well worn, hardly more than a skeleton leaf.

Take-Your-Time settled down, his back paws just over the edge of the pool, as it was still very hot, and listened.

"Once upon a time," began his great-grandpapa:

In a little burrow in a river bank lived a family of water shrews. It's Sherbert we're talking about now - the eldest lad, an adventurous little body. Now, just along the bank there was an Otter - quiet sort of chap, seemed friendly enough; but you can never be sure with someone so much bigger and stronger, and Sherbert and his family kept out of his way as a rule.

One evening, Sherbert had gone out into the river to look for caddis flies (and any other delicacies he could find), and he quite forgot how far he had come from home. Coming up to the surface, he discovered to his horror that he didn't seem to recognise anything.

"Help!" he squeaked. "Father! Hatty, Wylan, Huish!" But his squeak was carried away on the evening breeze and no one heard him.

Suddenly, away to his right, there was a loud slithering noise, followed by a splash-plop! It was a familiar sound: Otter, feeling playful, had whooshed down his mud slide into the river. At first, Sherbert was even more frightened: Otter was in the river too, and

he'd better look out. But then he realised something else. Otter had come from his house - over to the right - so that meant that *his* house must be over to the right too, only not so far. Taking care to wait until Otter had turned away downstream, Sherbert headed for where his home must be, and a few minutes later was getting a good scolding from his mother.

"Now you might suppose," More-Haste-Less-Speed addressed his great-grandson pointedly, "that the young mischief had learned his lesson. Oh no. Not him. Couple of days later, what does he do? Exactly the same, only this time it's later, and Otter's already out, so there's no help from that quarter."

"So what happened?" asked Take-Your-Time eagerly.

"I was about to tell you," said his great-grandpapa, turning the leaf over very slowly and gently. "All in good time!"

Sherbert swam and dived quite happily for some time before he realised he'd done it again. He couldn't see anything he recognised - in fact, he couldn't see much at all. He must have got into a current which had carried him quite a way - but which way?

Sherbert swam round and round in frantic circles until he was quite dizzy. "Mustn't panic," he told himself. "I mustn't panic!"

Suddenly he caught sight of a sleek, dark form moving rapidly through the water. Otter! For a moment he thought of running away; but he was too small, and too exhausted from swimming in so many circles. So, gathering up all his courage, he cleared his throat and, as the Otter came close, squeaked out "Oh, Mr. Otter, please Sir, can you most kindly tell me the way home?"

Otter paused and looked at him sharply. His eyes were very bright and his muzzle sleek and shiny. But his voice, though a little abrupt, was quite gentle as he said, "I know you, young Sherbert. Neighbours, almost, aren't we? Long way from home, my lad!"

"Which way?" asked Sherbert timidly.

Otter pointed back the way he'd come. "Never make it," he said with a glance at Sherbert's desperately paddling forepaws. "Climb up. Give you a lift!"

Sherbert wasn't sure if he was awake or dreaming as Otter helped him onto his broad tail and they set off upstream. Once Otter paused and sniffed; then, with a grunt that sounded like "Men!" he quickened his pace so that they fairly shot through the water. Nor did his family believe him when, safely lowered outside his own front door, he bounced in to tell them. His mother sent him straight to bed - "Telling stories as well!" she scolded.

But perhaps it was just as well, because it meant that Sherbert didn't see what happened to Otter as he swam back past his own front door. "Told you he'd be back," said a harsh, triumphant voice from the bank. "*Got* him!"

"Pity," said Sherbert's father when they realised there was no more Otter in their part of the river. "Seemed a quiet enough sort of chap. Still, must admit I feel safer."

But Sherbert cried for days and days and refused to go out by himself; and he started to collect Otter stories, till all the family thought he was mad. But Sherbert knew better.

Take-Your-Time hoped his

great-grandpapa hadn't noticed the tear that splashed into the pool. They both sat for a long time without speaking. There seemed nothing to say.

Then Take-Your-Time started slowly for home.

It wasn't till he arrived at his own front door that he remembered something - the invitation: still tucked safely into his shell . . .

Sherbert and his family were afraid of Otter because he was bigger and stronger; they didn't understand how much he cared for them.

God is much bigger and stronger than we are: but we need not be afraid of him, because he loves us very much.

Jesus told a story about a shepherd who had a hundred sheep, but he lost one. He left the ninety-nine to graze, while he searched everywhere for the one who was lost. The shepherd might even have died while he was looking for the sheep: Jesus said that "the good shepherd is willing to die for the sheep".

Did Otter know that the men would catch him? If so, why do you think he went on?

Jesus knew he was going to die on the Cross: but he went on, because he knew that was the only way to save us from the punishment for all the wrong things we have done.

He is the Good Shepherd, who died for us, his sheep.

5

Hedgehog Law

"Really, you'd forget your shell if it wasn't glued on!" Take-Your-Time's mother wasn't really very cross; she often forgot things herself (all tortoises do, that's why their shells are glued on), so she couldn't be.

"You'd better get up very early in the morning, go and give great-grandpapa the invitation, and bring him straight back with you!"

Take-Your-Time sighed; he'd have sore feet for days. But he couldn't very well complain, as it was his fault in the first place.

And so, very early the next morning, before the dewdrops had fallen, or Take-Your-Time's eyes would stay open properly, he set out for More-Haste-Less-Speed's sycamore tree.

"No dawdling, mind!" called his mother. "No scuffling in wet grass, no wandering after lettuces, and No Stories till you get back!"

"No, no, no," grumbled Take-Your-Time, but not loud enough for his mother to hear.

It was lunch time when he reached the sycamore tree, and his great-grandpapa had just begun a light snack.

"Sit down, sit down. Help yourself!" He waved a foot vaguely at the greenery around. “You’re early today.”

Take-Your-Time helped himself and explained why.

“A visit! How very kind.” More-Haste-Less-Speed looked a little apprehensive. “And we’re expected - er - at once?”

Take-Your-Time nodded reluctantly. “No-dawdling-no-scuffling-in-wet-grass-no-wandering-after-lettuces-and-no-stories-till-you-get-back!”

More-Haste-Less-Speed choked on his dessert. “Mothers!” He twinkled at his great-grandson. “But where would we be without them, eh lad?”

“But why do they always say no, no, no, great-grandpapa?”

More-Haste-Less-Speed wagged his head. “Oh, it’s a hard life, to be sure . . . it’s true, the answer isn't in the no's - but the no's have to be there, or you wouldn't be able to understand the yeses. Now, let me think . . . just fetch me my keys, there's a good lad."

Take-Your-Time certainly wasn't going to tell his great-grandpapa again about the No Stories; he settled down, his aching feet dangling in a puddle, and half-closed his eyes as More-Haste-Less-Speed began:

The hedgehogs were in a complete tizzy. Such a thing had

never been known! When old Spike had come back the first time and told them about The Boy, - well, he was getting on a bit and they hadn't taken too much notice. But this time, too many of them had seen and heard; it had to be true.

"But how come you could understand what he said?" demanded Hodge, an elderly, greying hedgehog who had always been a sort of unofficial leader among the Shed group.

"I don't really know," confessed Prickle, one of the younger members of the excited group with Spike. "I'm not even sure if he was talking our language - but I'm sure about what he said!"

Old Hodge shook his head. "It can't be as easy as that," he

muttered; then, glaring round at all the younger hedgehogs who, at one time or another, had been his pupils, he added sternly "And don't you be led astray, young hedgepigs! We all know about the Shed -

Builded wide, builded tall,
Never a window in its wall;
Never a door for man or pig,
Builded on stone 'gainst
them who dig."

The young hedgehogs nodded at the familiar rhyme.

"And what's inside the Shed, Pincushion?" Old Hodge loved to play schoolmaster.

"Bread and milk, Sir," said Pincushion promptly. "And fresh dry

leaves, and none of those horrible noisy machines!"

"Yes, yes." Prickle and the others shuffled and snorted impatiently. "We know all that - and The Boy said it was true - about what's inside - and a whole lot more! But it was the *other* thing he told us that was different: how to get in!"

Hodge withdrew his head a little and stiffened his spines.

"Impossible, I tell you. There's no way in, except what we've always known: no stealing someone else's supper, no tripping up the blind and elderly, no spiking your neighbour and no scratching against the Shed. You'll see, just follow the rules, and we'll find ourselves inside one day!"

"No, no, no," said Prickle

impatiently. "Why can't you believe there's a door and a key? It's so much easier!"

"Did you see it?" Hodge poked his head out again for a minute.

"Well, not exactly," admitted Spike. "But I'm sure we would have done," he added, half to himself. "Once we'd taken the key The Boy offered . . . yes, I'm sure we'd have seen the door then . . ."

Pincushion shuffled over and curled up next to Hodge.

"I think it's silly," she said. "What would The Boy want to help us into the Shed for? It must be a trap; he must want roast hedgehog for dinner. What does he know about the Shed anyway?"

"He said he built it," replied Prickle quietly.

Old Hodge drew back his head. "Too good to be true," he snorted.

"There's me - never stolen or tripped or spiked or scratched - must count for something, stands to reason . . ." And he rolled in a tight little ball away from the conversation.

Meanwhile Spike and Prickle were trying to collect a party to meet The Boy again the next evening; but, one by one, all the hedgehogs made excuses, and rolled off after Old Hodge. Spike looked round at the tiny group who had stayed with him, and his dim old eyes sparkled in the moonlight.

"You'll see," he said, his voice shaky with excitement. "Oh yes, you'll see!"

More-Haste-Less-Speed was

silent for so long that Take-Your-Time thought he must have finished. "And did they see?" he asked tentatively.

"See what?" said his great-grandpapa absent-mindedly.

"Inside the Shed," said Take-Your-Time. "The bread and milk and everything."

"Oh, more," said More-Haste-Less-Speed, carefully tucking the leaf into the bump in his shell. "Much more. But we must be off, lad, or your mother will have us in pieces with lettuce for supper. Come on, now, full steam ahead!" And he ambled off determinedly in the wrong direction.

Take-Your-Time chased after him. "This way, great-grandpapa! Great-grandpapa, was there really a door and did The Boy give them the key, just like that, for the asking?"

"Of course," said his great-grandpapa, changing course as Take-Your-Time nudged his shell. "Now, save your breath - you'll need it!"

Take-Your-Time obeyed.

Jesus told a story about a man who prepared an enormous feast and went to ask people to come to it. But, one after the other, they all made excuses, just like the hedgehogs. It all seemed too good to be true!

Jesus said that we cannot get to heaven by keeping a lot of rules - by "being good". He said that everyone who *believed in him* would go to heaven. Heaven is a gift from God to everyone who believes in Jesus.

Sometimes it seems that being a Christian is just a long list of things we must and must not do. (Can you remember some of them?) But we must remember that the most important part is what God has done for us: all the things that we do for him are to say thank you.

6

The Fox who wouldn't Forgive

It wasn't long before Take-Your-Time's mother began to wish she hadn't asked great-grandpapa to stay. Not that he was any trouble - really; but he was so slow! Everything seemed to take twice as long - including Take-Your-Time's bedtime stories. But when she mentioned it to his father, Time-and-a-Half merely looked surprised and said:

"Well, what's the hurry? Tomorrow's as good as today - probably better. World goes much too fast nowadays: stop worrying!"

Take-Your-Time was enjoying himself immensely: he even began to look forward to bedtime. And More-Haste-Less-Speed, though he always protested that he liked his own things round him, liked a captive audience even better, so he was enjoying himself too.

"Right, my lad," he would say, as Take-Your-Time snuggled down into the grass and dry leaves. "What shall it be tonight?"

"Have you got a story about a fox, great-grandpapa?"

And More-Haste-Less-Speed rummaged around in his shell and produced a reddish-brown leaf with crinkly edges.

"Once upon a time," Take-Your-Time peered over his great-grandpapa's shoulder.

"Now, it doesn't say that," More-Haste-Less-Speed glared at him. "We'll have you reading in a while - but don't you go making out you can do summat when you can't! Don't do any good in the Long Run."

Take-Your-Time blushed - as much as a tortoise can - and retreated under the bedclothes.

As Fritz sauntered along the hedgerow, you'd have thought he hadn't a care in the world. But that wasn't quite true. In fact his brain was working away busily, trying out all sorts of stories.

"I could tell Wolfem that I'll pay him when Aunt Foxglove dies and leaves me all her money . . . or when I've finished writing my book and sold it for thousands of pounds - except that I haven't

started it yet . . . or that I'll go and see Cousin Bulstrode tomorrow and borrow the money . . . But he wouldn't believe me - he's too clever."

Fritz snapped impatiently at a

butterfly and fidgeted with his watch.

"Oh dear, what *am* I going to tell Wolfem? I'll have to tell him something, he won't give me any more time to pay . . . perhaps it would be better to tell him how all the children will have to go barefoot, and my wife will have to go cleaning other people's holes and we'll all have to eat rotten vegetables and raid dustbins . . . Oh *dear*, here I am . . ."

Wolfem came out to meet him. Although his nose was sharp and his teeth pointed, his shaggy grey fur and a hint of sadness in his bright dark eyes made him look a little less fierce. But to Fritz, he was the most terrifying creature he'd ever seen.

"Well?" Wolfem could see how things were straight away. "You haven't brought my money, have you?"

All the fine stories Fritz had thought up flew clean out of his head. Hardly knowing what he was doing, he threw himself down at Wolfem's feet, his nose buried in his paws.

"Mr. Wolfem, Sir, I'll tell you the truth - I haven't got it, and I don't know where to get it. All the family fortunes put together wouldn't come to £20, let alone £100; as it is, the children haven't enough to eat and my wife hasn't had a new coat for six winters."

"He peered anxiously up at Wolfem. "But I *will* pay it, if it takes me the rest of my life - even if I have to live out of dustbins! Just give me time, Mr. Wolfem, please Mr. Wolfem - oh please, Mr. Wolfem, don't kill me!"

Wolfem gazed down at him, his bright eyes sad. He took a deep breath.

"Get up, Fritz," he said at last. "You'll never be able to pay me - you know that. If it was five pounds - maybe; but £100 - never. It would be no use giving you more time - now would it?"

Fritz shook his head slowly, not daring to look at Wolfem

"So there's only one thing to be done," continued Wolfem solemnly. Fritz waited, trembling. "I'm going to forget you ever owed me £100," said Wolfem quietly. "We'll start all over again, as if nothing had happened."

At first Fritz couldn't believe his ears. *Forget* it? All his anxiety and fear disappeared in a flash and he jumped up in excitement.

"Oh thank you, Mr. Wolfem, Sir! I'll do *anything* for you, Sir, anything you say! And I'll tell everyone how kind and generous you are!"

He danced back along the hedgerow, leaping twisting, frolicking for joy, batting the butterflies playfully, jumping over molehills.

But suddenly he remembered something. He stopped, changed

direction and, with a frown on his face, he strode purposefully into the next field.

"Cousin Freda!" He knocked abruptly at a little wooden door. An anxious little face peered out.

"That two pounds you owe me, or I'll have you for mufflers!"

"Oh Fritz, give me just another few days - I'll be paid on Friday, and then you shall have it - it's only been three days!"

"Not another minute! I know your sort! Out - come on, out! And don't you dare show your face round here again!" And he chased her across the field and into the wood, snapping angrily at her heels.

"How horrible!" Take-Your-Time sat up in bed indignantly. "After all Wolfem had done for him!"

"Ah," More-Haste-Less-Speed tucked the story into his shell. "But they did say that Wolfem's missus was seen in a nice bit of fox fur the next day, just the colour of Fritz's tail."

Jesus told a story about a servant who owed his master a lot of money, but his master decided to forgive him and not make him pay it back. But the servant went straight to another servant who owed him a few pence, and demanded his money. His master was furious, and threw the first servant into prison.

We can't expect God to forgive us if we don't forgive other people. Jesus also told us to pray

"Forgive us our trespasses (sins) as we forgive those who trespass against us".

What sins should we ask God to forgive us?

Are there things we should forgive other people?

When Peter asked Jesus how often we should forgive other people, Jesus said "Seventy times seven" - which meant, all the time!

7

Rabbit-Brained

Take-Your-Time was in disgrace.

He had been sent on an errand; a Very Important Errand, as his mother had told him several times. He had been sent to buy some extra strong buttercup juice to cure his great-grandpapa's rheumatism, as More-Haste-Less-Speed had been feeling it badly now that autumn was on its way.

Take-Your-Time had set off full of purpose and even speed; but then he met his friend Easy-Does-

It, who said why didn't he come on a beetle hunt - so Take-Your-Time went. And by the time they'd given up, they were both exhausted and Take-Your-Time had forgotten all about buttercup juice.

His mother came in. "Now, you're to go and apologise to great-grandpapa, and tell him you'll go first thing in the morning," she scolded. "First thing! Then to bed with you."

Take-Your-Time sidled nervously up to his great-grandpapa.

"I'm sorry, great-grandpapa," he said in a small voice. "I didn't mean to forget - I know it's important - only I met Easy-Does-It, and. . .and. . .but I'll go tomorrow, first thing!"

More-Haste-Less-Speed shifted his back legs with difficulty and twinkled at his great-grandson, though he said severely "So I should think! No sticking power, no concentration - here one minute, gone the next - that's the young nowadays. Rabbit-brained!"

"Why rabbit-brained, great-grandpapa?" Take-Your-Time thought he glimpsed the shadow of a story.

More-Haste-Less-Speed sighed. "Jump into bed, and I'll tell you."

Once in a burrow lived four rabbits: Feather and Dither, Slither and Sam. Each morning their mother would pack them all off to school, where the old schoolmaster rabbit, Sable, would read to them from The Books and make them recite what they'd learned the day before. But one day, when the time came for them to leave for school, Feather turned round to his mother and said:

"We're too old to go to school now; we're going to do what we want to from now on!"

Their mother twitched her ears and whiskers anxiously. "Well, yes, I suppose you are growing up now. But remember everything Sable taught you from The Books!"

"Yes, mother!" chorused Feather, Dither, Slither and Sam. "Of course we will!"

"The Books are right and true
and good

And teach us to live as we should," began Sam.
"Learning such good and useful habits
As become young growing rabbits," joined in Dither and Slither. Feather, whose memory was absolutely shocking, studied a passing butterfly carefully.

"Off you go then!" said their mother. "Make sure Sable would be proud of you!"

And the four young rabbits scampered off, chasing each other's tails, their own shadows, and a passing honey bee until they were quite exhausted and rather hungry.

"This is better than school," remarked Dither. "What's for dinner?"

At that moment, Feather appeared, dragging a large head of

lettuce. "Where did you get that?" The others gaped at him.

"Farmer Marrow's Fields," said Feather proudly.

"But Sable said it was wrong to steal," said Sam quietly.

"Oh dear!" Feather rubbed his whiskers with a grubby paw. "I clean forgot! But it's a lovely lettuce," he added. "Come on, everyone!" And he and Dither and Slither attacked the lettuce, whiskers quivering. But Sam contented himself with a clump of dandelion leaves nearby.

After dinner they played tag and hopscuttle and hide and seek . . .and it was while they were playing hide and seek that they lost Dither. Feather had hidden - under some leaves in the middle of a hollow hedge - and Slither and Sam had found him quite easily. But Dither was nowhere to be seen. In fact, he had been trotting along the edge of the field, a little behind the others because he couldn't make up his mind which way Feather would have gone, when he almost bumped into a large, grey rabbit, rather moth-eaten around the ears.

"Have a carrot?" The grey rabbit produced two or three from a large leaf under his arm. "Go on, I've got plenty."

Dither hesitated. The only place carrots grew was in Farmer

Marrow's vegetable patch.

"Sable said stealing was wrong," he blurted out.

For a moment the grey rabbit

looked angry. Then he said "Sable said. . . but you're old enough now to do what you like, not what Sable said. . . you like carrots, don't you?"

Dither nodded.

"Well then, take it! They'll only rot in the vegetable patch, they never get picked in time - go on!" And he thrust the carrot into Dither's wavering paw. "See you around!" And with a flash of his greyish tail, he was gone.

Dither soon found the others and shared the carrot with Feather and Slither; but Sam was beginning to see that it wasn't going to be easy to do what Sable said, and he promised himself that when he got home, he would read through all his schoolbooks, just to remind himself what Sable *did* say.

find the time has come for me to retire to my burrow. My eyes are growing dim, and I don't hear as well as I did. And I want you to take over from me!"

"So Sam became Top Rabbit," concluded More - Haste - Less - Speed, " and taught all the young

rabbits about The Books. But you remember what happened to the others," he looked sternly at Take-Your-Time.

"Yes, great-grandpapa. But I won't forget again, honestly I

won't - I'll bring the buttercup juice tomorrow - extra strong!"

"Buttercup juice, tchah!" More-Haste-Less-Speed creaked from side to side as he reached to put the story away. "The Books, that's what matters in the Long Run! Don't forget The Books! Ahem! Not that I'll say no to the juice, you understand. . ."

And he shuffled stiffly off to fetch his hot water bottle.

Do you know the story Jesus told about the farmer sowing his seed? Some fell on the path, and the birds ate it; some fell on stony ground, and the plants died because they hadn't enough water; some fell among thorns and weeds, and they grew up and choked the plants; but some fell on good ground, and the plants had lots of fruit.

The seed is like God's word; some of us hear it and forget it, like Feather; some of us hear it, but we let other people stop us from obeying it, like Dither; some of us hear it, but think other things are more important and go round with people who don't care about it, like Slither; but some of us hear it and obey it, like Sam: these are God's children.

It can be hard to follow Jesus and do what we know is right: what did Sam do to make it easier?

alighting heavily on the blackberry bush. "Rescue me, hide me! If my wicked uncle catches me, he'll beat me and starve me - and this heat'll be the death of me! Oh! and he's not far behind, please Mr. Sheldon, oh! oh!" And the bush swayed as she rocked backwards and forwards in despair.

It wasn't that Sheldon couldn't hear; but he was just about to slide away into a beautiful dream; and he didn't like butterflies - silly, scatterbrained creatures, never stopped talking; and it was just too hot to move. Slowly, very slowly, he drew his nose right back under his shell and lay very still. The butterfly flew clumsily down from the blackberry bush and fluttered over him. Sheldon didn't move.

"Oh! Oh! asleep, and I *can't* shout any louder. Oh dear, oh! What am I to do?"

And she flew slowly away, her light brown wings beating heavily. She hadn't gone very much further when her strength failed completely, and she collapsed on the edge of the path with a feeble "Oh!"

fly beat its way past, giving Wellcum a superior glance.

"That's him!" said the butterfly when Wellcum described him.

"OK, it should be safe for you to come out now," Wellcum wriggled his shoulder to give the butterfly room to crawl out.

But when she did, Wellcum could hardly believe his eyes.

Whether it was the elderberry juice or the extract of buttercup or being pressed next to his shell for so long, he couldn't tell; but the butterfly was no longer a light brownish colour all over, but the most beautiful mixture of reds, oranges, yellow, black and blue, all in a lovely pattern. He gazed at her.

"What's the matter?" asked the butterfly anxiously. "Am I all creased?"

"Go and look at yourself," said Wellcum. So they went to the edge of the stream and looked.

The butterfly gasped. "But how - who - is that really me?"

Wellcum nodded.

"But - I'm beautiful! And my wicked uncle will *never* recognise me now! Oh, thank you, Mr. Wellcum!"

And she flew happily away over the trees, the hedges and the blackberry bush where Sheldon lay asleep.

"And that was how Sheldon missed having a butterfly named after him," More-Haste-Less-Speed finished. "It was Wellcum who went down in all the books as being Assistant Creator of the Tortoiseshell Butterfly."

Take-Your-Time twisted his head and tried to inspect his shell.

"You've got that shell for a purpose," said his great-grandpapa. "Several purposes, in fact - so you just make sure you use it right!"

"Yes, great-grandpapa!" Take-

Your-Time turned to go. "And one day I shall have lots of stories to keep in it, just like you, great-grandpapa!"

Jesus told a story about three servants; their master gave each of them some money - lots of money to the first servant, quite a lot to the second, and a little to the third. The first two servants used the money to make more money for their master, but the third servant hid his money in case he lost it. Their master was very pleased with the first two servants, but furious with the third.

God has given to all of us things that we can do well - maybe you're good at looking after the baby, or reading - and he doesn't want us to hide them; we must use them!

But how?

Sheldon *did* use his shell - but who for? What about Wellcum?